BUILD YOUR OWN ADVENTURE

MEET ED

Brave Ed is a heroic firefighter in the LEGO® City fire department. It is his job to respond to all the emergencies that happen within the city. Ed's job is very busy and varied. He helps out at accident scenes, carries out rescue missions and, of course, fights fires!

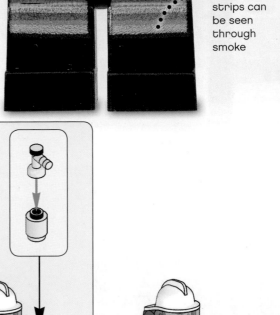

Standard-issue white fire helmet

Protective visor

Gauge shows air levels in oxygen tank on Ed's back

Breathing apparatus

Handy hook for rescue missions

Reflective strips can be seen through smoke

CITY HELPER

Ed is called out to many jobs around the city. This burning barbecue has got out of control, so Ed rushes to the scene carrying a handheld pump. The flames are extinguished in no time at all!

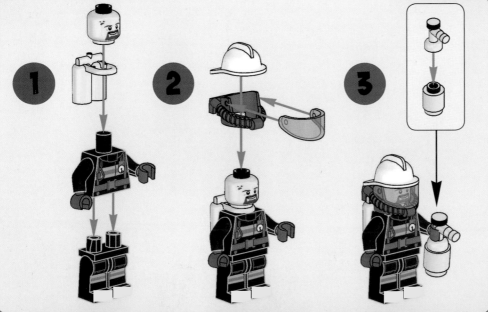

1

2

3

ED'S FIRE TRUCK

When the fire department receives an emergency call, Ed is often first on the scene in his small and speedy truck. Its bright lights signal to everyone that help is on the way.

Emergency blue lights

Windscreen

Yellow headlights

Wheel arch protects the truck from damage

PLENTY OF ROOM

Everything Ed needs for an emergency call can be stored in or on his fire truck. His handheld pump clips to the side, and other equipment fits inside the side lockers or on top of the truck.

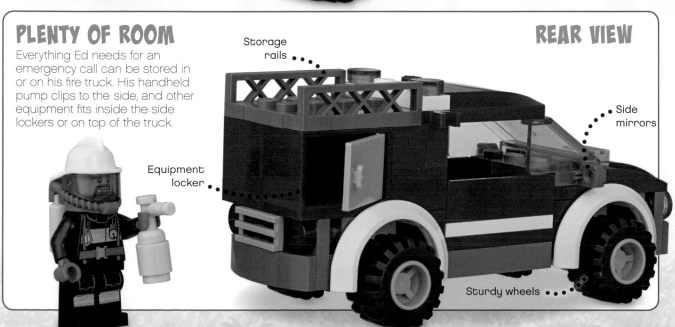

Storage rails

REAR VIEW

Side mirrors

Equipment locker

Sturdy wheels

FIRE TRUCK INSTRUCTIONS

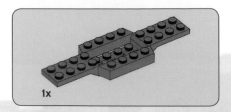

1x

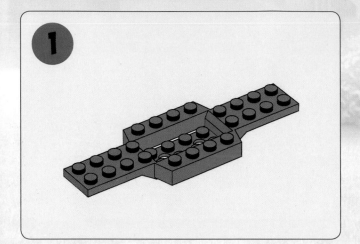

1

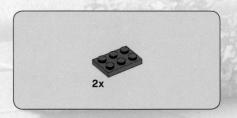

2x

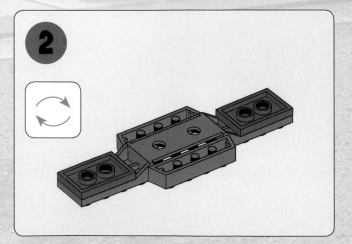

2

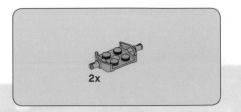

2x

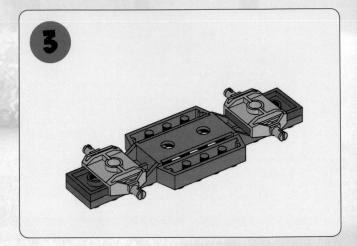

3

LET'S GET BUILDING!

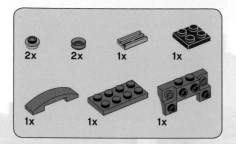

2x 2x 1x 1x

1x 1x 1x

1

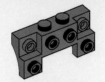

2

3

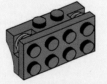

4

5

6

4

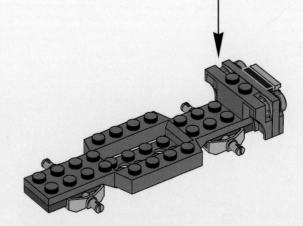

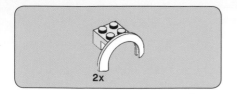

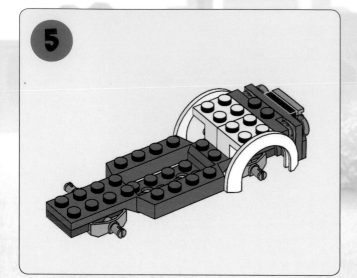

5

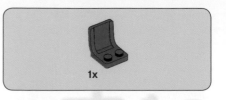

7

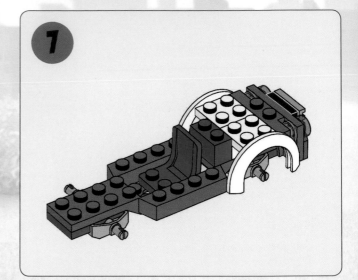

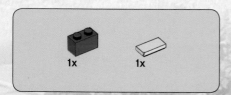

6

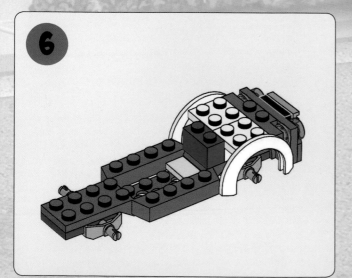

8

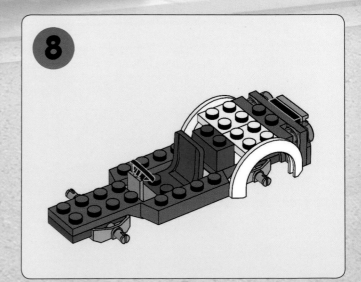

2x

1x

1x 1x

1x

ARE THE WHEELS ATTACHED? OVER.

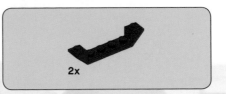

2x

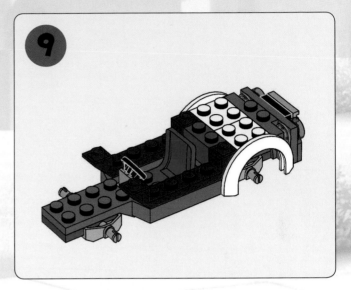

9

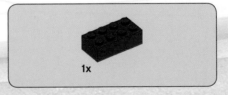

1x

10

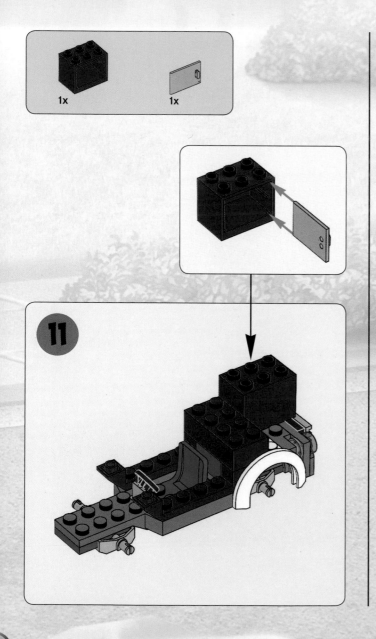

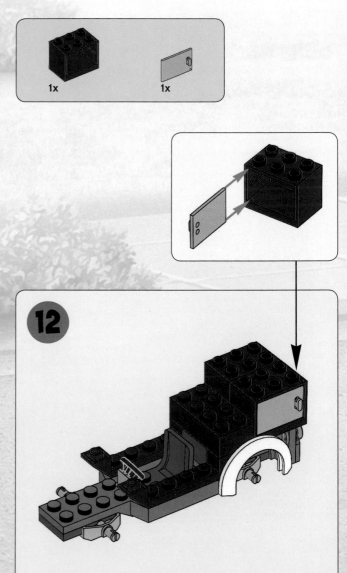

YOUR BUILDING SKILLS ARE ON FIRE!

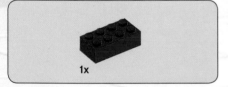

1x

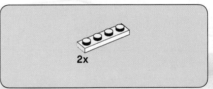

2x

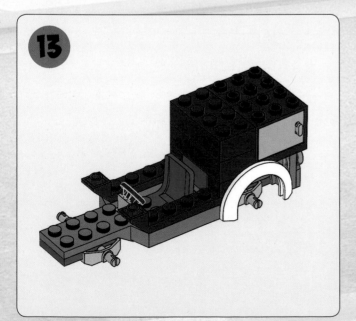

13

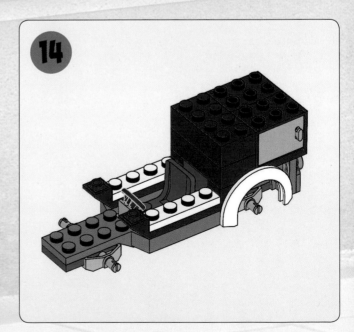

14

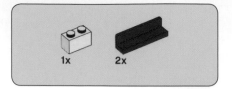

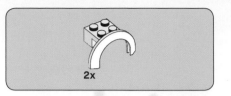

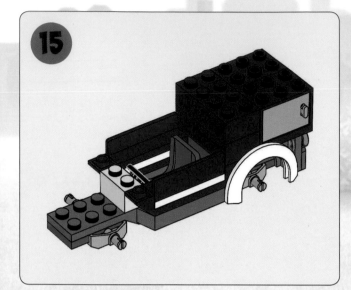

15

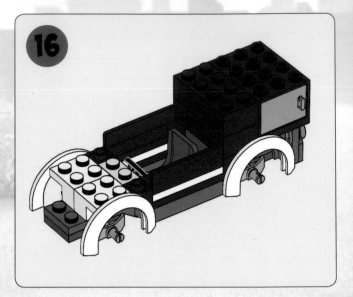

16

WHERE ARE THOSE WHEELS?

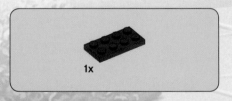

17

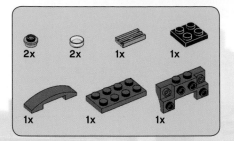

1

2

3
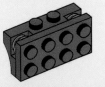

4

5

6

18
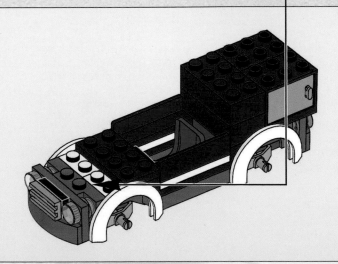

19

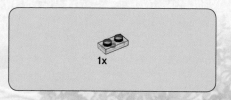

20

21

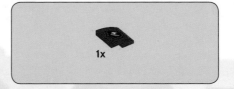
1x

23

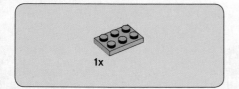
1x

22

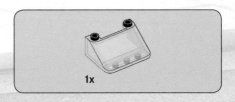
1x

24

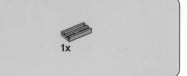

1x

25

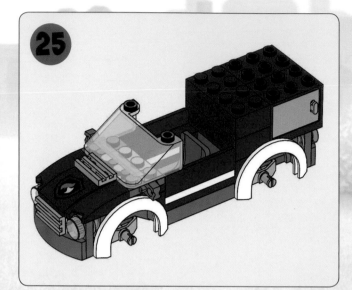

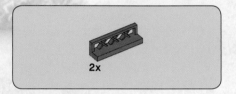

2x

1x

26

27

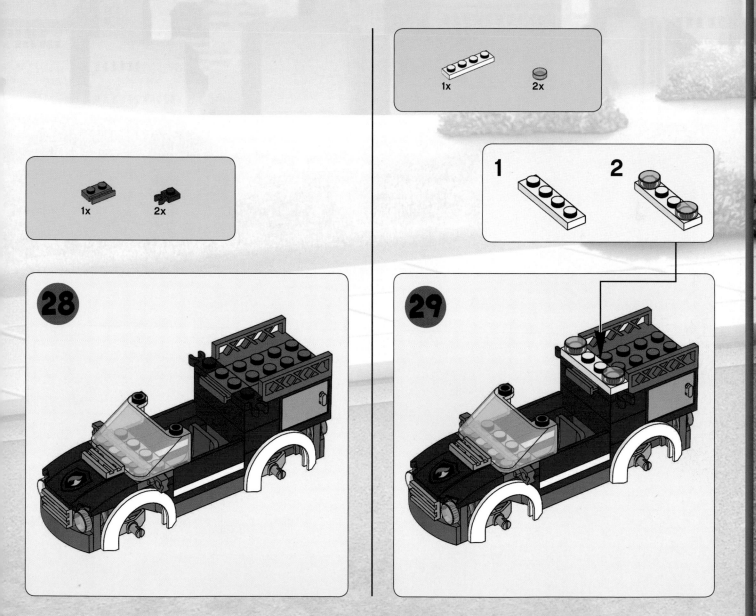

28

29

1x   2x

1x   2x

1   2

30

31

1x

4x 4x

4x

READY TO ROLL!

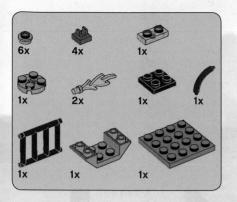

6x 4x 1x
1x 2x 1x 1x
1x 1x 1x

1

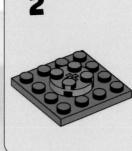

2

3

4

5

6

7

8

32

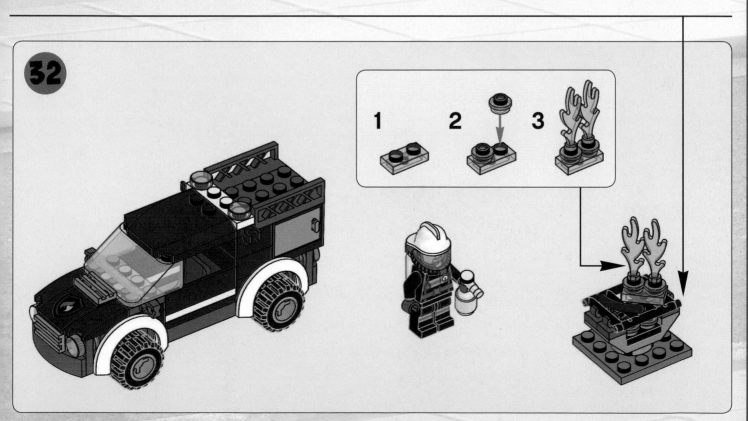

1   2   3

BUILD YOUR OWN ADVENTURE

In the pages of this book, you will discover an exciting LEGO® City adventure story. You will also see some clever ideas for LEGO City models that might inspire you to create your own. Building LEGO models from your imagination is creative and endlessly fun. There are no limits to what you can build. This is your adventure, so jump right in and get building!

HOW TO USE THIS BOOK

This book will not show you how to build the models, because you may not have exactly the same bricks in your LEGO collection. It will show you some useful build tips and model breakdowns that will help you when it comes to building your own models. Here's how the pages work...

PERHAPS YOU COULD BUILD ME A TV?

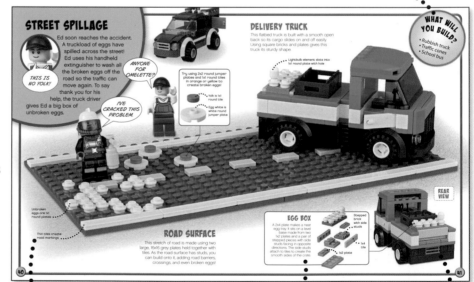

"What else will you build?" flashes give you even more ideas for models you could make

Special features or elements on models are annotated

Breakdowns of models feature useful build tips

Sometimes, different views of the same model are shown

18

HELLO, I'M ALICE FINCH.

MEET THE BUILDER

Alice Finch is a LEGO fan and super-builder, and she made the inspirational LEGO models that can be found in this book. To make the models just right for the LEGO City world, Alice worked with the LEGO City team at the LEGO Group headquarters in Billund, Denmark. Use Alice's models to inspire your own amazing models.

BEFORE YOU BEGIN

Here are five handy hints to keep in mind every time you get out your bricks and prepare to build.

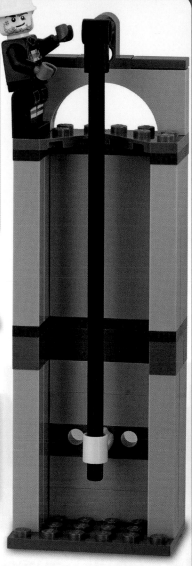

Organise your bricks
Organising bricks into colours and types can save you time when you're building.

Be creative
If you don't have the perfect piece, find a creative solution! Look for a different piece that can create a similar effect.

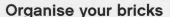

COMPLETING PRE-BUILD CHECKS...

Research
Look up pictures of what you want to build online or in books to inspire your ideas.

Have fun
Don't worry if your model goes wrong. Turn it into something else or start again. The fun is in the building!

Make your model stable
Make a model that's sturdy enough to play with. You'll find useful tips for making a stable model in this book.

WHAT A GREAT HAUL!

BUILDER TALK

Did you know that LEGO® builders have their own language? You will find the terms below used a lot in this book. Here's what they all mean...

STUD

Round raised bumps on top of bricks and plates are called studs. A string has a single stud at each end. Studs fit into "tubes", which are on the bottom of bricks and plates.

2x2 corner plate

String with studs

MEASUREMENTS

Builders describe the size of LEGO pieces according to the number of studs on them. If a brick has 2 studs across and 3 up, it's a 2x3 brick. If a piece is tall, it has a third number that is its height in standard bricks.

1x1 brick

1x2 brick

2x2 brick

2x3 brick

1x1x5 brick

CLIP

Some pieces have clips on them, into which you can fit other elements. Pieces such as ladders fasten onto bars using built-in clips.

1x1 plate with vertical clip

1x1 plate with horizontal clip

Flag with two clips

HOLE

Bricks and plates with holes are very useful. They will hold bars or LEGO® Technic pins or connectors.

1x1 brick with hole

2x3 curved plate with hole

2x2 round brick

1x2 brick with two holes

4x4 round brick

SIDEWAYS BUILDING

Sometimes you need to build in two directions. That's when you need bricks or plates like these, with studs on more than one side.

1x4 brick with side studs

1x1 brick with two side studs

1x2/1x4 angle plate

1x1 brick with one side stud

Ladder with two clips

BRICK

Where would a builder be without the brick? It's the basis of most models and comes in a huge variety of shapes and sizes.

2x3 curved brick

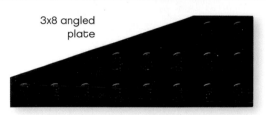

2x2 brick

 1x2 brick

 1x1 headlight brick

 2x2 domed brick

1x1 brick eye

 1x2 grooved brick

 1x1 round brick

PLATE

Like bricks, plates have studs on top and tubes on the bottom. A plate is thinner than a brick – the height of three plates is equal to one standard brick.

3x8 angled plate

2x3 plate

1x2 jumper plate

1x8 plate with side rail

2x2 round plate

1x1 tooth plate

1x1 round plate

4x4 curved plate

4x4 round plate

TILE

When you want a smooth surface to your build, you need to use a tile. Printed tiles add extra detail to your models.

1x6 tile

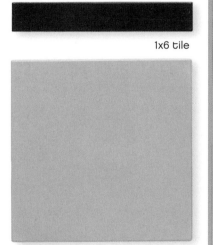

2x2 tile

2x2 tile with pin

6x6 tile

1x2 printed tile

SLOPE

Slopes are bigger at the bottom than on top. Inverted slopes are the same, but upside-down. They are smaller at the bottom and bigger on top.

1x2 slope

1x2x3 inverted slope

HINGE

If you want to make a roof that opens or give a creature a tail that moves, you need a hinge. A ball joint does the same job, too.

1x2 hinge brick and 1x2 hinge plate

Hinge plates

1x2 hinge brick and 2x2 hinge plate

Ball joint socket

2x2 brick with ball joint

Hinge cylinder

1x2 plate with click hinge

21

RISE AND SHINE

Ding-ding-ding-ding! Firefighter Ed is dreaming about his bright red fire engine and its loud emergency siren. But wait – that's not the sound of a fire engine. It's Ed's alarm clock! Ed wakes up in his room above the fire station, ready for another busy day at work.

GOOD MORNING!

LAMP

A tall lamp stands on one side of Ed's bed. It has a big blue shade and a cord hanging down so that Ed can turn it on and off without getting up.

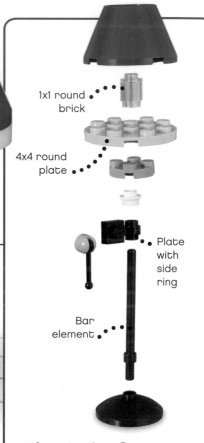

1x1 round brick

4x4 round plate

Plate with side ring

Bar element

Pull-cord is a joystick piece

Radar dish base

ALARM CLOCK

Turn a printed clock tile into an alarm clock with a pair of ice-cream pieces for bells. If you don't have these particular pieces, make a simple clock by fixing a printed tile to a 2x2 brick on its side.

CLOCK WORK

The alarm clock is built around a hub piece with four bars. Slot 1x1 round plates with holes onto two of the bars, then fit the ice-cream pieces onto these.

Hub with four bars

LEGO® Technic half pin joins hub piece and round plate

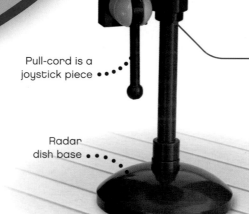

1x1 round plate with hole

Ice-cream piece

Printed clock tile

SWITCHED ON

The lampshade is a cone on a 4x4 round plate with a clear round brick for a bulb hidden inside. The lampstand is made of a bar element and a radar dish. A plate with a side ring connects the pull-cord to the stand.

BEDSIDE TABLE

The alarm clock stands on this bedside table, but is not attached to it. Tiles on top create a smooth surface, apart from one jumper plate that stops the clock from tipping forward.

BEDS

There are beds at the fire station for all the firefighters. Use a range of colourful bricks to create different sheets and pillows. Both of these beds are four studs wide and six studs long – perfect for a minifigure!

1x2 curved slopes cover a 1x4 plate to create pillows

1x1 round plate

1x1 round brick

Curved slopes make a cosy comforter

MAKE YOUR BED

Use 1x2 curved half arches to make the sides of the bed, with a 2x4 tile for a smooth top. A gap between the bedspread and the floor helps it look like a real bed.

2x4 tile

Base plate holds bars in place

1x2 curved half arch

Two-stud wide bricks form the base

1x2 slope makes a plastic pillow

I PUT THE "ED" IN BED!

Headboard is raised on stacked 1x1 round plates

1x4 curved bar with studs

ED'S BED

Ed sleeps in a bed with a black metal frame with curved bars at both ends. A brown base plate could be wooden floorboards or a brown carpet.

GETTING READY

Firefighter Ed is the first person in the fire-station bathroom each and every morning. The other firefighters are still snoozing in their bunks as he starts his speedy scrub. Ed washes his face at the sink and then jumps in the shower. The hot water wakes him up for the day ahead.

TIME FOR A SHOWER!

BATHROOM SINK

Everything Ed needs for his morning routine is attached to the bathroom wall using sideways building. The bright bulbs above the mirror light up Ed's smiling face. The red-and-white tiles match the rest of the fire station.

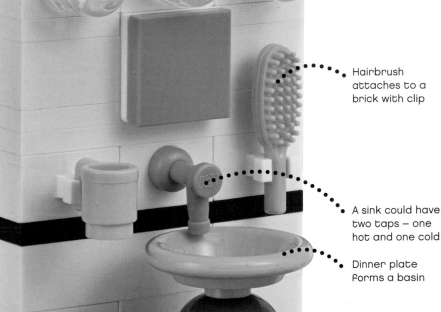

1x6 plate locks the wall together at the top

Lightbulbs are transparent minifigure heads

Hairbrush attaches to a brick with clip

A sink could have two taps – one hot and one cold

Dinner plate forms a basin

A round plate and a dome create the rounded base of the sink

Sturdy wall is built up from a small base plate

SIDEWAYS SYSTEM

Build with pieces that can help you attach things sideways to your bathroom wall. Bricks with holes are useful for this, as you can plug the stud of a piece straight into them, or insert a LEGO Technic half pin to attach something different.

Brick with hole holds lightbulb in place

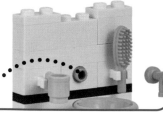

Angle plate attaches to mirror tile

LEGO Technic half pin attaches to tap piece

Shower stand is a bar attached to the wall with clips

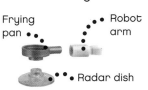

A few small pieces make a shower head with flowing water.

Frying pan •••

•• Robot arm

•• Radar dish

I AM A SOAPRANO SINGER!

CENSORED!

Different sized tiles create a patterned floor •

1x2 grille piece makes a shower drain

SHOWER

Ed loves starting the day with a song and a quick hose-down in the shower. His fellow firefighters try to avoid the bathroom while he is singing, which is lucky for Ed as the see-through shower curtain doesn't provide much privacy!

CREATING FOLDS

Rows of red hinged plates and 1x2 plates create the folding function of the shower curtain. The rest of it is made from transparent bricks and window pieces. More hinged plates attach the curtain to the wall.

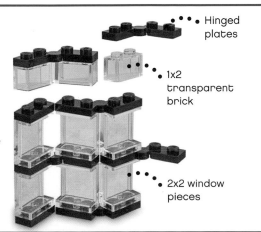

Hinged plates

1x2 transparent brick

2x2 window pieces

WHAT WILL YOU BUILD?
• Bathroom cabinet
• Bathtub
• Rubber duck
• Toilet

STATION ALARM

Ding-ding-ding-ding! This time, Ed knows he's not dreaming! The ring of the station alarm means there's been an emergency call. Ed checks the computer and finds out where he needs to go. Ed is so busy he doesn't hear the morning's news – some crooks have escaped from the local jail!

I HAVEN'T EVEN HAD MY BREAKFAST!

RADIO

Ed loves listening to music. But this morning, his favourite tunes are interrupted by news about a jailbreak. The news crackles out through the speaker, but Ed is too far away to hear!

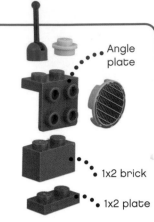

Green 1x1 round plate for "on" switch

Printed tile looks like a speaker grille plate

Angle plate

1x2 brick

1x2 plate

An angle plate, a 1x2 brick, and a 1x2 plate make the main part of the radio.

WORKSTATION

Ed's workstation is equipped with a computer and a cup of coffee. If only he had time to drink it! The table stands on 1x1 round bricks and 2x2 jumper plates.

CROOKS ON THE LOOSE!

A hinge brick with a printed tile creates a desktop computer.

1x2 hinge brick

Space for another walkie-talkie

Hinged plates adjust the angle of Ed's workstation

GEAR RACK

A row of bricks with clips makes an equipment rack. Build it into a larger unit and add emergency lights to fit the firestation theme.

Transparent pieces make emergency lights

Brick with horizontal clip

IT IS A LONG WAY DOWN!

FIREFIGHTER'S POLE

Sliding down a pole gets the firefighters from their bedrooms to ground level in no time. This pole is made from a long LEGO Technic cross axle. If you don't have a long axle, you could use LEGO Technic connectors to link shorter ones.

WHAT WILL YOU BUILD?

- Uniform lockers
- Town map
- Tool bench

Add bands of colour for variety

I'VE GOT HIGH HOPES FOR YOU!

1x4 brick with holes

The pole shaft's walls are locked together at the top with small red plates and strengthened using angled plates.

3x3 angled plate

Tall bricks create a more stable build than lots of short ones

Cross axle is 16 studs long

Angled connector

Pin-connector plate wih two holes

POLE POSITION

Fix the pole in place with LEGO Technic pins and LEGO Technic connectors. These fit into a pin-connector plate at the top of the wall and a brick with holes near the bottom of the wall.

LEGO Technic connector

LEGO Technic pin

LET'S ROLL

Ed leaps into his fire truck and starts the engine. As the station's automatic door cranks open, the fire chief calls out to him: "Good luck, Ed! I hear there are crooks on the loose!". But, once again, Ed doesn't hear the warning. He switches on his siren and heads for the road.

TAKE CARE, ED.

STATION GARAGE

Ed keeps his fire truck ready for action in the fire-station garage. This model uses special LEGO door pieces – though you can also build a garage without a door. Just make sure it is big enough for your fire truck to fit through!

1x8x2 bar element

Tall pillars are a quick way to create a structure without walls

I SAID, WATCH OUT FOR CROOKS!

Start building up the room from this large base plate

SIDE VIEW

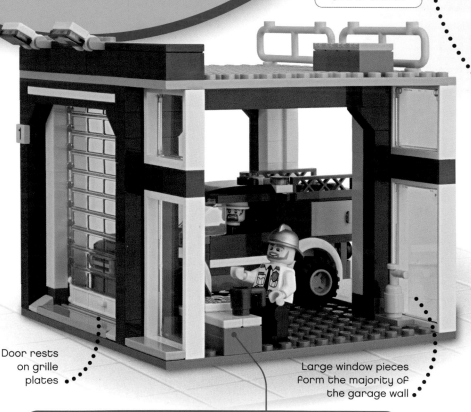

Door rests on grille plates

Large window pieces form the majority of the garage wall

Newspaper printed tile

The desk is topped with a mug, a printed tile and a phone. The phone is built around a headlight brick, which has studs on top and on the side.

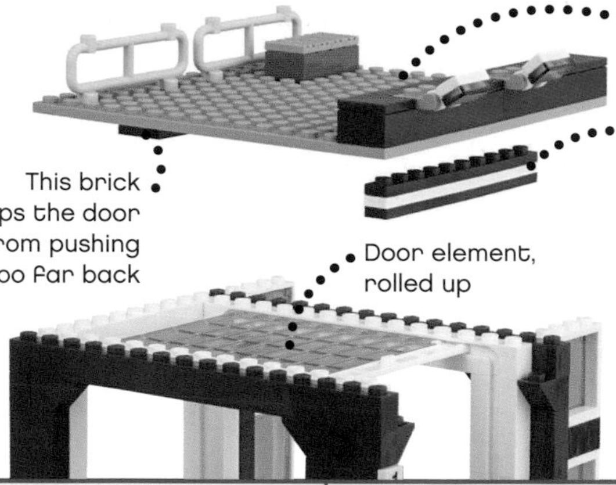

Large grey base plate forms a flat roof

Frame of red and white plates

This brick stops the door from pushing too far back

Door element, rolled up

DOOR WAY

The sliding door comes as one single element. Its special hinged panels fit into bricks with grooves. They allow the door to slide up and around into the roof.

WHAT WILL YOU BUILD?
• Briefing room
• Drill tower
• Staff canteen

Connect plates with clips and bars to make these adjustable lights.

1x2 trans-blue tile

1x2 plate with clips

1x2 plate with bar

1

DID HE SAY COOKS?

ON THE ROAD

Ed is on an early morning call-out in his fire truck. He loves his job, but right now all he really wants is some eggs for breakfast! With his lights flashing and his siren wailing, he drives quickly and carefully, watching out for traffic signals, roadworks and people going to work.

SIRENS REALLY WAKE YOU UP!

GOOD MORNING, CITY!

TRAFFIC LIGHTS

Ed keeps a careful eye on the traffic signals as he drives along the city streets. Use red, yellow and green plates to make your traffic-light model.

Radar dish

1x1 round plate

Brick with side stud

LIGHT UP

Three bricks with side studs make the main part of these traffic lights. They attach to the top of a piece with a stud at one end and a 2x2 base at the other. A small radar dish attaches to the very top.

ZEBRA CROSSING

Help your minifigures cross the road safely with this pedestrian crossing. You don't need one long grey piece to make it – the white pieces can hold smaller grey ones together.

White 2x4 tile

ROADWORKS

Ed isn't the only one up early! These workers are mending holes in the road before it gets too busy. They have built a wooden frame to hold their dry cement and are mixing it in with sand and water to make sticky concrete.

Wheel

Pin connector plate wih two holes

Turntable

Axle

Brick with cross hole

Smooth tiles create wooden planks around the cement pit.

Three 2x6 bricks fill the frame

Shovel held by plate with top clip

CEMENT MIXER

The mixer drum tips from side to side using the wheel, which fits onto a LEGO® Technic axle. The axle threads through a number of pieces with specially designed holes. The drum also rotates on a 2x2 turntable. If the cement inside the mixer stops moving, it will set hard!

8x8 grey base plate holds the frame and cement together

LET'S MIX THINGS UP!

Wheel turns the inner axle

Cone

Handle is the perfect size for minifigure hands

Base is built around a 2x6 plate

1x2 tile gives a smooth surface for the drum to rest on

Each pair of wheels is a single element

MARKET MAYHEM

Poor Ed! Everything he sees on the road makes him even hungrier for breakfast. There's a baker's cart selling croissants... There's a fruit stall full of bananas... There's even a chef selling ice creams! Ed doesn't have time to stop this morning, though. He has an important job to do!

NO TIME FOR A CROISSANT.

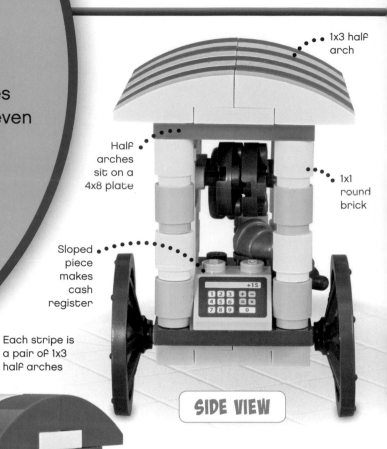

1x3 half arch

Half arches sit on a 4x8 plate

Sloped piece makes cash register

1x1 round brick

+15
123+-
456x%
789 0

SIDE VIEW

Each stripe is a pair of 1x3 half arches

BAKER'S CART

This eye-catching cart uses blue and white pieces to make a stripy awning on stripy poles. Pastries hang on a display rack in the middle of the cart. If you don't have ready-made food pieces, a 2x2 round plate makes a giant bagel!

Brown 2x2 round plate hangs on bar

A short bar piece slots into a brick with side stud to make a simple stand.

Old-fashioned wheels

Window frame creates a stand

Pre-made crate piece adds detail to the scene

Inverted cone

Mailbox

Angle plate

Tiles create smooth surface

Plate with side studs

SIDEWAYS SCOOP

The base of the freezer trolley is made from a red plate, topped with yellow tiles. Two mailbox pieces lie sideways on the smooth tiles. They attach to the base build with a grey angle plate.

Wheel piece

HEY! COME BACK HERE!

ICE-CREAM TROLLEY

This cycling chef rides around town towing a cool refrigerated trolley. It attaches to a clip on the back of the bike, so check the height of your bike before you start building.

Freezers are mailboxes with hinged doors

4x4 round plate

Plate with bar

Crate piece

Hinge brick

Hinge bricks underneath the crates allow them to stay in place while also tilting forwards.

GREENGROCER'S STALL

There are lots of healthy breakfast options on offer at this fruit and vegetable stall. The pineapples are the same shape as minifigure heads and have green flower pieces on top.

Sign clips to a single post and base piece

FRUIT AS BIG AS YOUR HEAD!

Grey base plate looks like the pavement

TRAFFIC JAM

THERE'S NO TIME TO LOSE!

Ed knows he is close to the emergency scene when he reaches a traffic jam. The LEGO City Police have put barriers across the road and now there is a big line of cars. When the other drivers see and hear Ed's fire truck, they are happy to pull over to the side of the road to let him pass.

STANDING STRONG

Both barriers stand on a pair of 3x4 angled plates, but they are attached differently in each case. The red legs bend up and down using a clip-and-bar connection, while the grey legs rotate around a ball-and-socket connection.

Plate with clip

3x4 angled plate

1x2 plate with bar

3x4 angled plate

Plate with socket

1x2 plate with ball

ROADBLOCKS

City commuters can't miss these brightly coloured barriers. The barriers warn drivers to slow down well in advance of the accident.

PLEASE FORM AN ORDERLY LINE.

2x6 plate

3x4 angled plate

1x8 plate

Joints allow barriers to fold flat

1x1 tile

3x4 angled plate

WHAT WILL YOU BUILD?

- Speed camera
- Road signs
- Road bridge

SPORTS CAR

With its green go-faster stripes, this car looks like it's moving even in a traffic jam! The car uses many similar pieces to Ed's fire truck, but looks completely different!

COMING THROUGH!

I HOPE I'M NOT LATE FOR MY LUNCH MEETING!

Windscreen is one moulded piece

1x1 transparent slopes make sleek angled headlamps

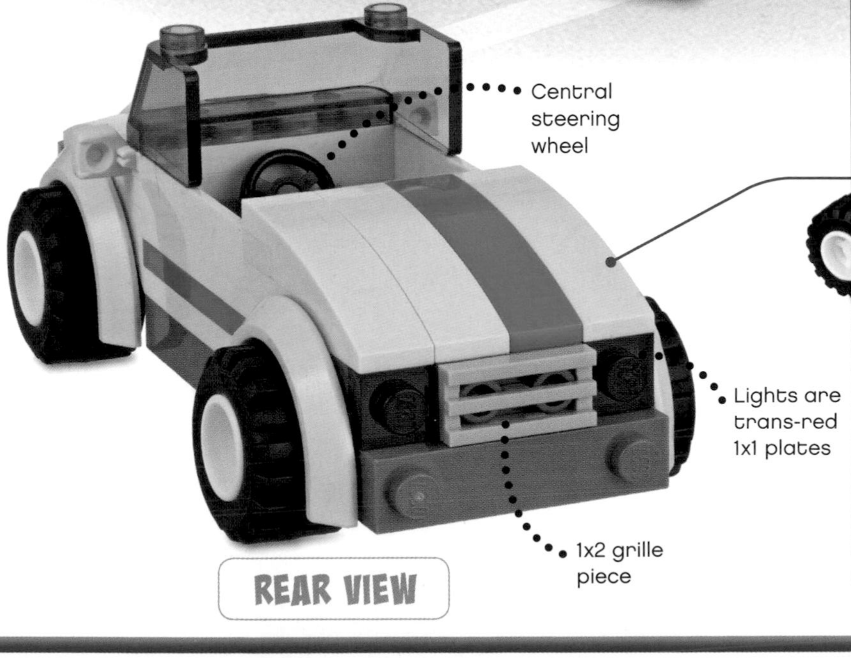

Central steering wheel

4x12 chassis plate

2x2 plate with axles

Lights are trans-red 1x1 plates

1x2 grille piece

REAR VIEW

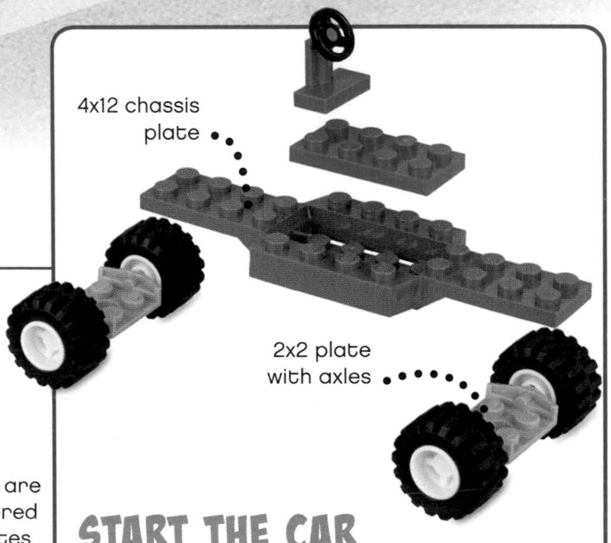

START THE CAR

A chassis piece, which is also in Ed's fire truck, makes the base of this sports car. This is attached to two pairs of wheels, and filled in with a 2x4 plate with a steering wheel on top.

STREET SPILLAGE

Ed soon reaches the accident. A truckload of eggs have spilled across the street! Ed uses his handheld extinguisher to wash all the broken eggs off the road so the traffic can move again. To say thank you for his help, the truck driver gives Ed a big box of unbroken eggs.

THIS IS NO YOLK!

ANYONE FOR OMELETTE?

I'VE CRACKED THIS PROBLEM.

Try using 2x2 round jumper plates and 1x1 round tiles in orange or yellow to create broken eggs!

Yolk is 1x1 round tile

Egg white is white round jumper plate

Unbroken eggs are 1x1 round plates

Thin tiles create road markings

ROAD SURFACE

This stretch of road is made using two large, 16x16 grey plates held together with tiles. As the road surface has studs, you can build onto it, adding road barriers, crossings, and even broken eggs!

DELIVERY TRUCK

This flatbed truck is built with a smooth open back so its cargo slides on and off easily. Using square bricks and plates gives this truck its sturdy shape.

WHAT WILL YOU BUILD?
• Rubbish truck
• Traffic cones
• School bus

Lightbulb element slots into 1x1 round plate with hole

REAR VIEW

EGG BOX

A 2x4 plate makes a neat egg tray. It sits on a level base made from two 1x2 plates and a pair of stepped pieces with side studs facing in opposite directions. The side studs attach to tiles to create the smooth sides of the crate.

Stepped brick with side studs

1x4 tile

1x2 plate

41

IN THE KITCHEN

EGG-CELLENT WORK, ED!

Ed's fellow firefighters are delighted to see him return to the station with more than enough eggs to feed them all. They tell him to relax on the sofa while they cook him a big breakfast of sausages and eggs. Soon he will have all the energy he needs for the day's next adventure!

KITCHEN SURFACES

This kitchen is built for feeding lots of hungry firefighters! It has lots of ovens, a fridge and a big countertop with a built-in chopping board. There is even a blender for fruit smoothies and two taps for hot and cold drinks.

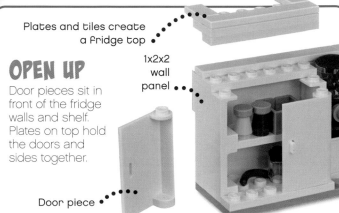

Plates and tiles create a fridge top

OPEN UP
Door pieces sit in front of the fridge walls and shelf. Plates on top hold the doors and sides together.

1x2x2 wall panel

Door piece

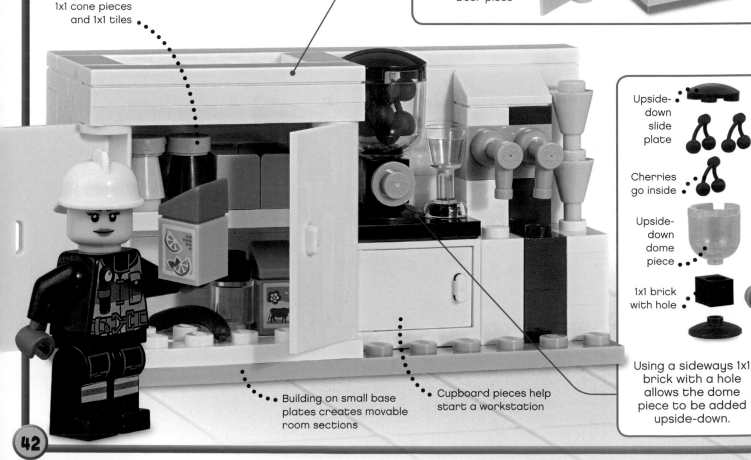

Make jars out of 1x1 cone pieces and 1x1 tiles

Building on small base plates creates movable room sections

Cupboard pieces help start a workstation

Upside-down slide plate

Cherries go inside

Upside-down dome piece

1x1 brick with hole

Using a sideways 1x1 brick with a hole allows the dome piece to be added upside-down.

SOFAS

These seats are made from smooth tiles and curved pieces to give them a comfy, padded look. The red armchair has two 1x3 plates for feet, while the blue sofa uses four 1x1 round tiles.

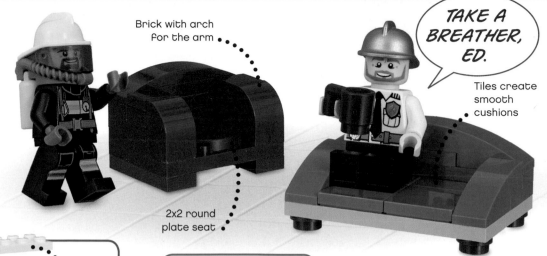

Brick with arch for the arm

TAKE A BREATHER, ED.

Tiles create smooth cushions

2x2 round plate seat

Wall element

2x4 plate

Cupboard doors

EASY PIECEY

Two wall elements make the back of the cupboard, with pre-made doors on front. A 2x4 plate on top locks them together.

Pre-made drawer unit

1x1 round plate

1x1 round plates make hobs for the top of these ovens. Try using red plates to show which burners are on.

WHAT WILL YOU BUILD?
- Dining table
- Vending machine
- Kitchen sink

Mugs fill the serving hatch

I THINK I NEED A BIGGER PAN!

Mailboxes serve as ovens

43

IN THE PARK

It's a sunny day in the city, and the best place to enjoy it is in the big park. There are fountains and play areas, and lots of trees and grass. But that's not why three escaped crooks have come here. They're looking for the loot they buried before they went to jail!

LET'S GO SOMEWHERE SHADY!

WHAT A GREAT HIDING PLACE...

Roof is made of stacked slope bricks

Floor of play area is a 6x8 black plate

2x2 turntable

CREATE A CAROUSEL
The park's roundabout is built on a 6x6 round plate, with four chair pieces attached. The carousel spins on a 2x2 turntable with 1x2 tiles around it.

Ladder is one element

PLAY AREA
All the children in the city love this play area. The crooks are lucky there are no kids around right now, as they find their loot buried beneath the slide!

6x6 round plate spins on turntable

16x16 green base plate

BUILD A BASE

The ladder and slide of this playground are both single pieces. The plates at the top of each combine with long plates to create a frame for the top part of the model. This all sits on tall 1x1x6 bricks.

MY TROUSERS ARE WET!

Transparent blue crystals and 1x1 round tiles stack to make the water jets.

Crystal with central stud •••••

Row of 1x2 grille pieces •••••

Transparent blue 4x10 plate •••

6x12 base plate ••••

WHAT A GREAT SLIDING PLACE!

FOUNTAINS

There are lots of water features in the park. Water jets spring from a shallow pool, rising to different heights and glinting in the sunshine. The taller fountain has taps for people to drink from.

Tap clipped into 1x1 brick with side studs ••••

Loose translucent 1x1 round plates create water ••••

5x5 radar dish ••••

Cone piece •••••

Wheel hub ••••

Telescope ••••

Radar dishes ••••

1x1 round bricks ••••

DELICATE DETAILING

Use large pieces to begin your builds, then add small and unusual-looking pieces of the same colour to create an elaborate fountain.

BARBECUE BLAZE

The crooks have found their buried treasure. To celebrate, they head for the park's picnic area and start up one of the barbecues. But they are so busy counting their stolen loot that they don't notice the grill going up in flames and setting fire to a nearby tree. Look out!

I'M A CROOK, NOT A COOK!

WHAT A PLEASANT DAY OUT.

1x6 curved bar

1x2 grille

Perfectly cooked chicken

1x2 tile with top bar

Flower with open stud

BBQ RECIPE

The griddle base is a 1x6 plate and a 2x6 plate, with two 1x3 bricks for feet. The red cooking area is made of two grilles and four flowers on top of a 2x4 plate.

Small flames slot into flower pieces

Safety barrier

You could use two separate, smaller base plates

PICNIC BENCH

The seats and the table of the bench are one build. The bench legs are 1x3 bricks which support the arch bricks that attach to the tabletop.

1x4 curved arch

1x3 brick

PICNIC AREA

This big outdoor table has room for six people to sit and enjoy a picnic. The benches and tabletop are all made from brown plates. These thoughtful picnicers keep careful watch on their own griddle.

TREE FIRE

This tree has a seating area all round its base and now flames all over its canopy of leaves! You can decorate LEGO® leaf pieces with lots of different details – try flowers for a springtime tree with blossom.

Large flames are out of control!

Flame connects to open studs on the leaf pieces.

2x2 round plate with four vertical bars

BRANCHING OUT

Green leaf pieces branch off a 2x2 round plate with four vertical bars. This plate sits between the trunk and a 1x1 round brick at the top of the tree trunk.

CALL 999!

Build this model with your giveaway bricks! (see p.17)

NO, DON'T DO THAT!

Tree trunk is a 1x1x6 column

SIMPLE BENCH

Build a simple bench with just a few pieces

1x1 round brick is one of four legs

BENCH BASE

The trunk is attached to a 2x2 jumper plate in the bench base. This is surrounded by four 2x2 tan angled bricks, and sits on top of a bench made of brown curved plates and a round brick.

2x2 jumper plate

2x2 angled brick

3x3 curved plate

RAISE THE ALARM

Just moments after the crooks have fled the scene, the park ranger rides by the picnic area on her bike. As soon as she sees the fire, she pedals back to her ranger's hut as fast as she can to raise the alarm. She dials 999 and asks for the fire department.

WE'LL BE RIGHT THERE!

RANGER'S HUT

This simple cabin has a phone for emergencies and a flag on top so visitors to the park can find it easily. It is open on one side, so it doesn't need a door.

1x2 ridged slope

Plates create the base of the roof

Grey pieces are plates with clips holding details within the model

Shutters clip onto bricks with side clips so they can open and close.

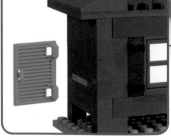

THERE'S NO TIME TO LOSE!

Hut sits on 1x2 bricks at the front and 1x1 bricks at the back

REAR VIEW

Stacked bricks support the roof from underneath ●●●

Flagpole attaches to jumper plate ●

WHAT WILL YOU BUILD?
• Park gates
• Bird-watching hut
• Signpost

Phone attaches to brick with side studs built into hut wall

Plates with clips hold the park ranger's equipment

PITCH PERFECT

1x2 slope brick
2x3 slope brick
1x2 slope
1x1 slope

Differently pitched slopes create interesting roofs. This one uses larger slopes at the bottom, getting smaller towards the top.

PARK MAP

When the firefighters arrive, the park ranger will use this map to show them exactly where to go. It is built with printed map tiles, but you could use small tiles or plates to make your own map.

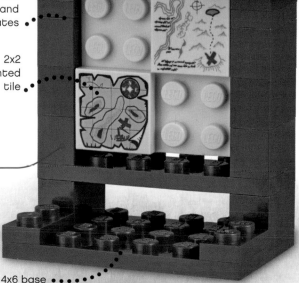

Roof sticks out to protect the map display from rain ●●●

Sides mix bricks and plates ●

2x2 printed tile ●●

4x6 base ●●●●

THAT'S THE WAY

Use angle plates to build the sideways front of the map. The angle plates sit on a 1x6 plate that bridges the gap between the two side columns.

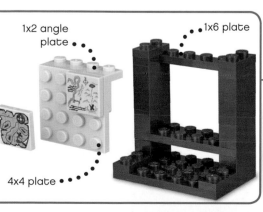

1x2 angle plate ●●

1x6 plate

4x4 plate ●●

PONDSIDE PUMP

When Ed gets to the park, the ranger sees that he has some special equipment with him. It pumps water from the nearest pond and straight onto the flames! It only takes a few minutes for heroic Ed to put out the fire on the grill, but no one can work out who started it...

I FEEL PUMPED!

LET'S GET OUT OF HERE...

WHAT WILL YOU BUILD?

- Topiary bushes
- Boardwalk
- Bandstand

Joystick lever acts as on/off switch

SIDE VIEW

2x2 dome

FIRST EGGS, NOW A BARBECUE. WHAT A DAY!

WATER PUMP

This electric pump looks so realistic because it doesn't have any visible studs on its shiny red body. It has an on/off switch, a pressure gauge and a cooling vent. It connects to two yellow hose pipes.

1x1 cone

NATURE POND

This peaceful pond is a haven for wildlife. Frogs hop among the reeds, rushes and lilies, while birds visit the feeder at the water's edge. Angled plates create the muddy banks and 2x2 round bricks make stepping stones.

Rush is made from a 1x1 round brick, a bar, and a 1x1 cone

Lilypad leaf is a green dish

BIRD FEEDER

This covered bird table is made from two window frames. Two plates with rails on top provide extra shelter. The two red slopes make an angled roof.

1x2 slope

1x2 plate with rail

Window frame

2x2 plate

1x1 round brick

4x4 angled plate

Rocky stepping stones emerge from the water

Blue 16x16 base plate

1x2 grille for cooling vent

Black connector is part of hose element

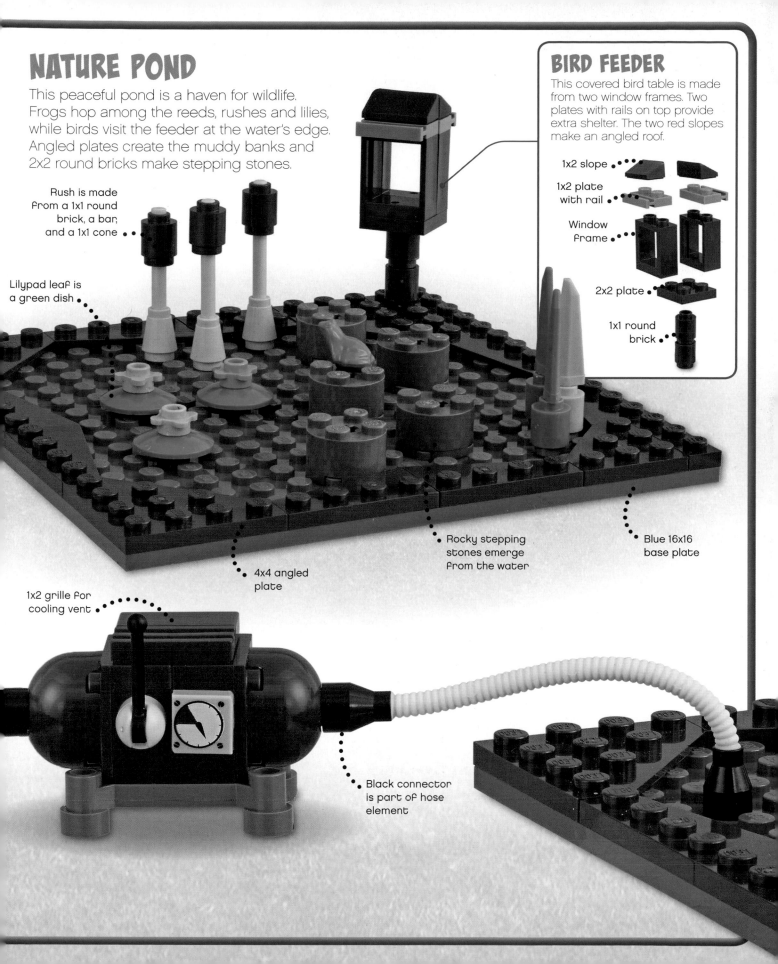

55

RECREATION ROOM

Heroic Ed has solved two problems already today, so he's ready to relax with his fellow firefighters. He likes reading and keeping fit, and he can do both at the fire station. Ed's earned this break, but he still has to be on alert. Another emergency call could come in at any moment!

TIME FOR TABLE TENNIS?

WHAT WILL YOU BUILD?
- Table football table
- Basketball hoop
- Pinball machine

Barbell is a ninja staff

Make your dumbbell heavier or lighter by adding or removing round plates.

Inner weight is 2x2 round plate

Barbell clips above for storage

Outer weight is 2x2 round tile with hole

Bench clips onto rack when not in use

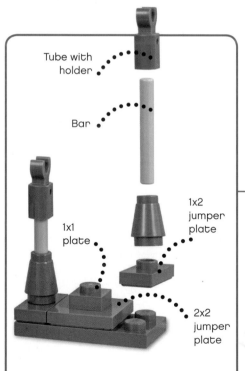

Tube with holder

Bar

1x1 plate

1x2 jumper plate

2x2 jumper plate

BARBELL RACK

The base of the rack is made from three jumper plates on a 2x4 plate. A 1x1 plate on the middle jumper plate connects it to the underside of the bench.

BENCH PRESS

Firefighters have to be fit, so Ed stays in shape by lifting weights. His bench is simply a 2x6 plate with tiles on top and log bricks for legs.

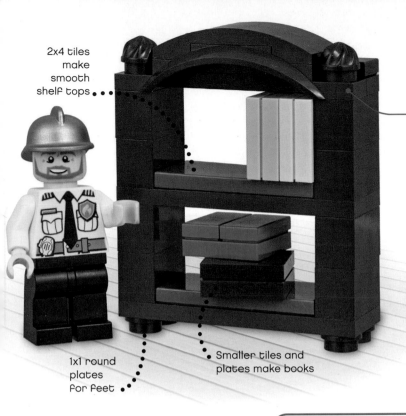

2x4 tiles make smooth shelf tops •••••

1x1 round plates for feet •••

Smaller tiles and plates make books

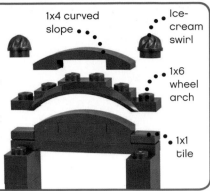

TOP TIP

A 1x6 wheel arch spans the front of the bookcase top. Use three plates to mirror its stepped shape at the back, then add two curved slopes for a smooth finish.

1x4 curved slope •••

Ice-cream swirl •••

1x6 wheel arch •••

1x1 tile •••

BOOKCASE

Using pieces in unusual ways can turn a simple build into something special. The carved details at the top of this bookcase are actually ice-cream pieces and a wheel arch!

TABLE TENNIS

Ed likes to challenge his fellow firefighters to a game of table tennis at least once a week. If Ed wins, he doesn't have to wash up for the rest of the day!

Fence piece •••

The net is made from two short fence pieces back to back.

1x1 plate with side clip •••

Bat clips into plate under table

THAT'S 10-2 TO ME!

6x12 plate table •••

1x1 white tile for ball •

Table leg is a telescope piece •••

Clip to hold bat •••

AT THE DOCKS

While Ed and the other firefighters relax at the station and wait for their next call, the three crooks are making trouble down at the docks. They need to get their stolen silver out of the city, and have spotted a raft that looks perfect for a silent escape by sea.

LET'S GET OUT OF HERE.

THE PERFECT GETAWAY.

DOCKSIDE

Sailors can moor their boats at this jetty, which extends from the shore into the deeper waters of the dock. It stands on tall wooden stilts made from 1x1 round bricks.

Sailors tie their boats to T-shaped metal bars called cleats. This one centres on a 1x1 brick with two side studs.

1x1 round brick

1x1 brick with side studs

1x2 jumper plate

Life preserver

Ladder for boarding boats at low tide

String with studs

Rubber tyre for boats to bounce off

Imagine the posts continue below the waves

WHY IS TREASURE SO HEAVY?

STOLEN SILVER

This chest is stuffed full of loot! Adding silver pieces to the top of plain grey plates creates a huge stack of swag for the crooks.

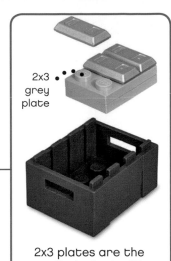

2x3 grey plate

2x3 plates are the perfect size to fit inside the chest.

PLANK PIECES

Two 1x8 plates hold stacks of log bricks together. An extra row of logs bricks on each end of the plates makes it look like the wooden logs are tied together with rope.

THIS CAN'T FAIL.

Oar piece

Log bricks are attached sideways

Sideways 1x8 plate

WHAT WILL YOU BUILD?

- Boathouse
- Lighthouse
- Buoy

WOODEN RAFT

With no loud engine to attract attention, this simple raft is ideal for a sneaky getaway. It is built out of brown log bricks to make it look like wood.

RIVER ROUTE

The crooks load their loot and start to row – but the silver is too heavy and cracks the raft! It starts to sink, leaving them no choice but to swim away. They scramble back to dry land, but without their precious cargo! A kind crane operator offers his help.

THIS PLAN HAS A HOLE IN IT!

LEAKY RAFT

Using the same basics as a normal raft, this raft has a hole that is the perfect size for the chest to slide into – plus water leaks springing up all over!

I'VE GOT A SINKING FEELING.

Chest is not fixed with studs

1x2 log brick

1x4 log brick

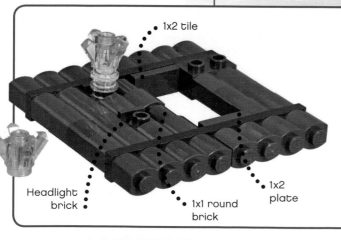

1x2 tile

1x2 plate

Headlight brick

1x1 round brick

MIND THE GAP

A 1x2 plate and a 1x2 tile make this gap exactly the right width for the chest. The water spouts fit into headlight bricks next to 1x1 round bricks.

WHAT WILL YOU BUILD?

- Lifeboat
- Warehouse
- Lorry

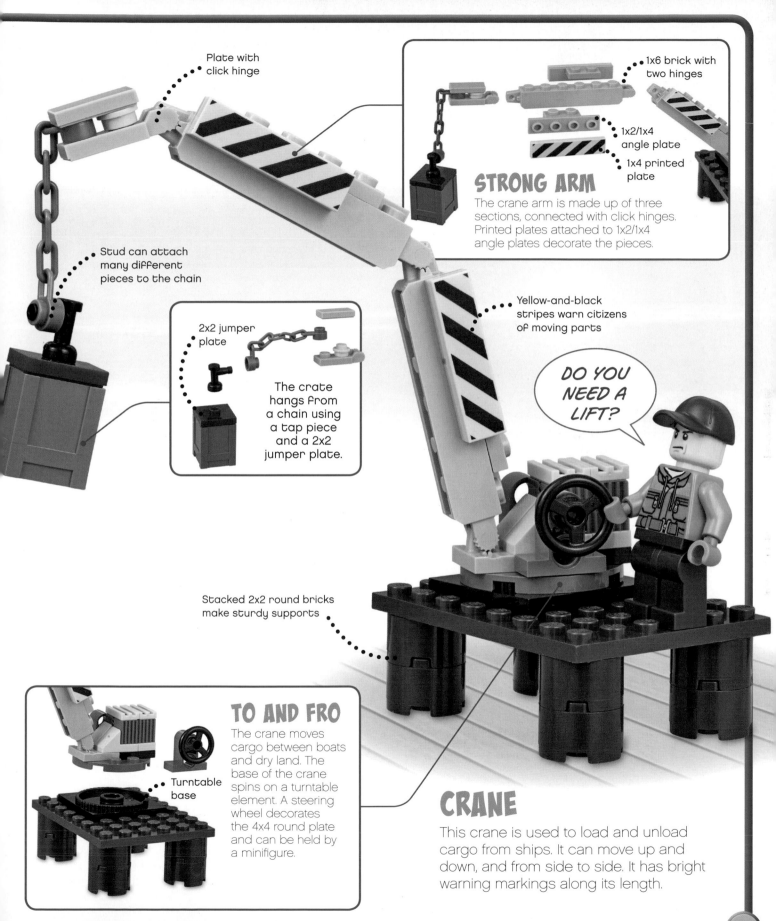

Plate with
click hinge

Stud can attach
many different
pieces to the chain

2x2 jumper
plate

The crate
hangs from
a chain using
a tap piece
and a 2x2
jumper plate.

1x6 brick with
two hinges

1x2/1x4
angle plate

1x4 printed
plate

STRONG ARM

The crane arm is made up of three
sections, connected with click hinges.
Printed plates attached to 1x2/1x4
angle plates decorate the pieces.

Yellow-and-black
stripes warn citizens
of moving parts

*DO YOU
NEED A
LIFT?*

Stacked 2x2 round bricks
make sturdy supports

Turntable
base

TO AND FRO

The crane moves
cargo between boats
and dry land. The
base of the crane
spins on a turntable
element. A steering
wheel decorates
the 4x4 round plate
and can be held by
a minifigure.

CRANE

This crane is used to load and unload
cargo from ships. It can move up and
down, and from side to side. It has bright
warning markings along its length.

SPY IN THE SKY

High above the docks, a helicopter is filming for the local TV station. When the pilot sees the sinking raft, he grabs his mobile phone and calls 999 right away. He also has time to get some good footage of the crooks to show on the evening news!

I SPY TROUBLE.

HELICOPTER

This chopper has to be very fast to get the day's news stories before anyone else. Vents cool its powerful engine, while its simple tail keeps its weight down and its speed up!

REAR VIEW

COCKPIT VIEW

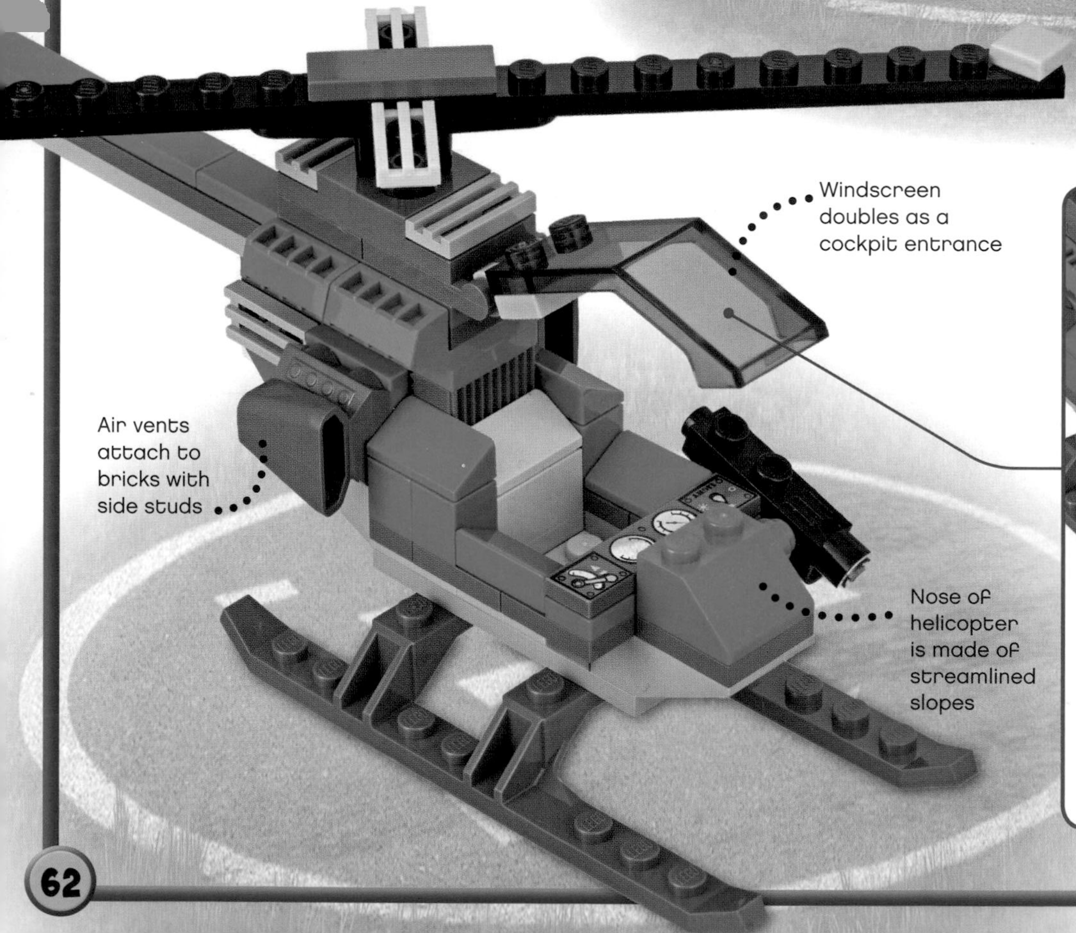

Windscreen doubles as a cockpit entrance

Air vents attach to bricks with side studs

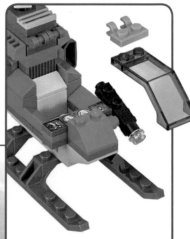

Nose of helicopter is made of streamlined slopes

A plate with side clips and a plate with handled bar allows the windscreen to lift up and reveal the cockpit.

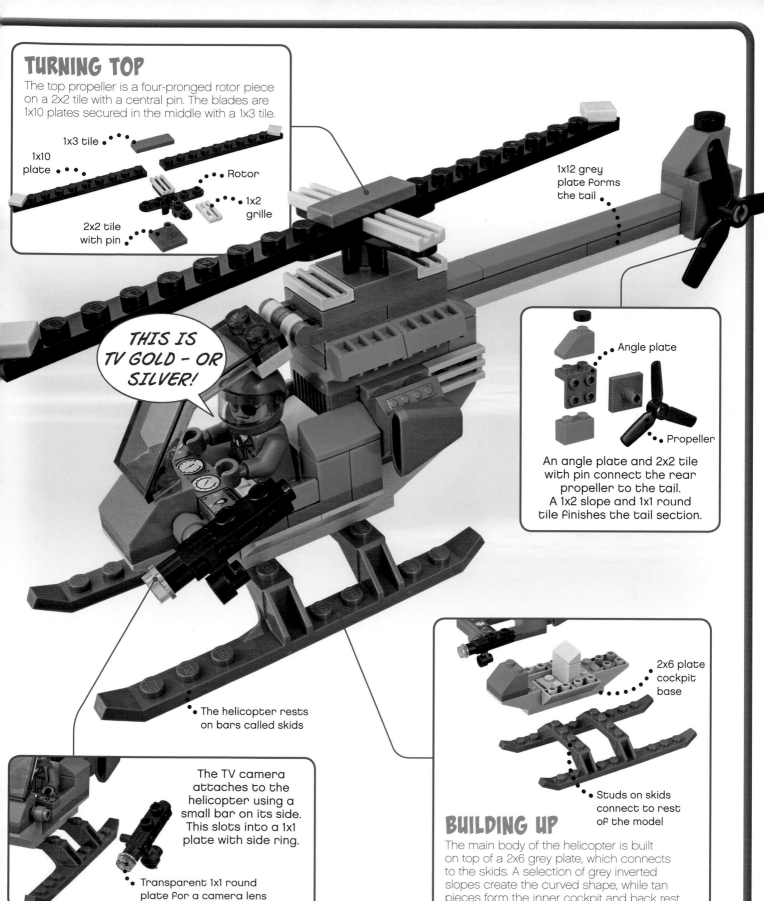

TURNING TOP

The top propeller is a four-pronged rotor piece on a 2x2 tile with a central pin. The blades are 1x10 plates secured in the middle with a 1x3 tile.

1x3 tile

1x10 plate

Rotor

1x2 grille

2x2 tile with pin

THIS IS TV GOLD - OR SILVER!

1x12 grey plate forms the tail

Angle plate

Propeller

An angle plate and 2x2 tile with pin connect the rear propeller to the tail. A 1x2 slope and 1x1 round tile finishes the tail section.

• The helicopter rests on bars called skids

The TV camera attaches to the helicopter using a small bar on its side. This slots into a 1x1 plate with side ring.

Transparent 1x1 round plate for a camera lens

2x6 plate cockpit base

Studs on skids connect to rest of the model

BUILDING UP

The main body of the helicopter is built on top of a 2x6 grey plate, which connects to the skids. A selection of grey inverted slopes create the curved shape, while tan pieces form the inner cockpit and back rest.

SEASIDE SUPPORT

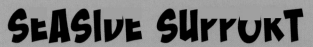

By the time Ed gets to the docks in his truck, the crooks have already run away and the silver has sunk to the seabed. The coastguard are patrolling the area in their dinghies, but they need the fire department's help to raise the silver back to the surface.

I HOPE I'M NOT TOO LATE TO HELP!

Steering wheel

2x2 angle plate

MOTOR ROTORS

The motors for both dinghies fit sideways onto angle plates that are attached to the studs on the back of the boats. Details are added to these plates to give a mechanical look to the models.

1x1 round plates on 1x2 plate with side rail

Why not add a flag to the front of your boat?

Step for getting in and out is a 1x2 grille

The motor's control is made from a robot claw fixed to a plate with a handled bar.

Plate with handled bar

IS IT FINDERS KEEPERS?

Controls on printed tile

DINGHIES

These large pieces work as boats on their own, but have studs for adding extra details, such as motors and steering gear. They also have bars on the sides for mooring them with string.

1x1 cone

FUEL STATION

The dinghies can fill up their engines at this pier. The fuel pump has a long hose made out of two tube pieces so it can reach down to the water level.

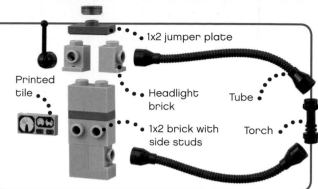

PUMP IT UP

The pump uses a 1x2 brick with side studs and three headlight bricks to add details to the front and side. The hose is two tubes connected by a torch piece.

Printed tile

1x2 jumper plate

Headlight brick

Tube

Torch

1x2 brick with side studs

LOOK OUT FOR THAT SILVER, LADDIE!

Joystick for on/off control

Transparent orange 1x1 round tile

Posts are stacked 1x1 round bricks

Small blue base plates are used to create rippling waves

WHAT WILL YOU BUILD?

- Boat ramp
- Speedboat
- Boat lift

SUNKEN TREASURE

Ed knows just the thing for rescuing the sunken silver. He gets into the fire department's speedy Jet Ski and lowers a string of floats into the water to mark the spot where the treasure lies. A fire department diver swims down to recover the silver. Mission accomplished!

READY, JET, GO!

REAR VIEW

Water sprays out of jets at rear

BUILDING UP THE BACK

Ed stands in front of the Jet Ski's engine, which is a 2x2 curved slope on an angle plate. He is protected from spray by a tile with top bar.

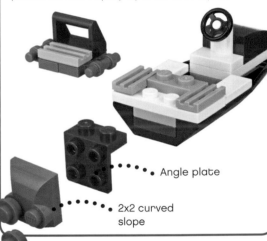

Angle plate

2x2 curved slope

Tile with top bar stops Ed falling backwards at high speed!

FINALLY, AN EXCUSE TO USE THE JET SKI!

Nose is two 1x3 curved slopes

JET SKI

Ed is ready for a water rescue with his Jet Ski. It is small and sleek so it can move faster and more easily than a bigger boat. Water sprays out from its rear as Ed whizzes across the water.

The underside of the Jet Ski is a single 4x6 hull piece. The rest of the model is built up from this base.

STRING OF FLOATS

Floats have lots of uses. They can mark boundaries, stop boats from crashing into piers, and even raise sunken treasure! These floats use just a few small LEGO pieces.

Strings with studs at both ends link the floats

The long floats are a stacked dome brick, a round brick and an inverted dome. They attach to a string with studs.

Notches on each string can be held in minifigure hands

WHAT WILL YOU BUILD?
- Diving bell
- Shipwreck
- Fire boat

SUNKEN RAFT

The raft and the stolen silver are waiting for the diver on the sandy sea floor. As soon as Ed gets hold of it, he can return it to its rightful owner – which definitely isn't either of these crabs!

The rocks on the seabed are made from two slope bricks, a headlight brick, and a corner plate. Plant pieces look as if they are swaying with the current.

- Corner plate
- 1x3 slope

Sea grass slots into 1x1 round bricks

16x16 base plate

1x1 round plates make shells and pebbles

Tools for Trouble

As the sun starts to go down, the three crooks are preparing for a night raid on the city's shops. They lost all their silver at the docks and they don't want to end the day empty-handed! They start by sneaking into a hardware store to get their hands on some tools...

THIS STORE IS A CROOK'S DREAM.

Plates with top clips keep items in place

HARDWARE STORE

This cluttered shop is piled high with tools for every occasion. There are buckets and buzz saws, paint rollers and power drills – but all these crooks want is a great big crowbar!

FRONT VIEW

ITS GOT EVERYTHING WE NEED!

Textured bricks have a wall pattern

The lamp is made from a brick with a snap connector, more often used to make arm and leg joints for robots!

Upside-down 1x1 round plate

Brick with snap connector

1x1 transparent round brick

BRACKETS

The top shelf is supported by pieces built into the wall. At the far ends, the supports are standard 2x2 bricks. In between the windows, 2x2 inverted slopes are used.

Tool box

DO WE NEED A FRYING PAN?

Printed tile tilts on hinge element

Chain wrapped around bar

SHOP FURNITURE

There are lots of tools on this rack, including the crowbar the crooks are after. The cash register has been left open for the night, to show there is no money to steal.

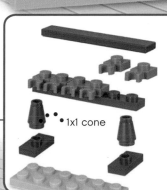

Plate with rail looks like open cash drawer

Crowbar

Blowtorch

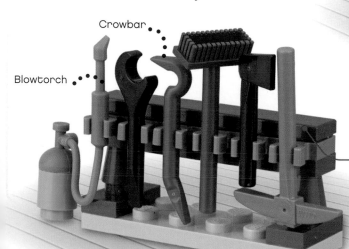

TOOL RACK

A row of plates with side clips is sandwiched between a 1x1 plate and a 1x6 tile to make this tool rack. The feet are 1x1 cones on jumper plates.

1x1 cone

KITCHEN TAKEOVER

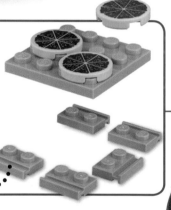

The crooks' next stop is a pizza parlour that has closed for the night. They won't find much to steal there, but boy, are they hungry! They put some pizzas in the oven, but don't know how long to cook them for. The next thing they know, there is smoke everywhere!

ANY FLAVOUR BUT BBQ!

PIZZA WARMER

This special cabinet can keep 12 tasty pizzas hot until they are ready to eat. It has three warming drawers that slide in and out on grooves built in to the sides.

Four smooth tiles on top

Plates with rails slot into the side grooves. The one at the front acts as a handle.

1x2 plate with side rail

Unit can be moved round the kitchen on two pairs of wheels

MAKE MINE CRISPY!

WHAT WILL YOU BUILD?
- Wood-fired oven
- Delivery scooter
- Coffee machine

The oven's chimney is a LEGO® Technic cylinder with a half pin inside. These are stacked on top of a dome piece.

PIZZA OVEN

Unbaked pizzas go into one end of this big oven and come off the conveyor belt at the other end perfectly cooked. At least, they do when a chef is in charge!

CONVEYOR BELT

The conveyor belt is all one element with a rotating handle and moving rubber belt. Arch bricks create curved openings at either end, but the rest of the model is a simple box shape.

Oven chimneys are soon filled with smoke!

1x2 grille slope

I'LL TURN UP THE HEAT.

Printed tiles attach to an angle plate

PIZZA PARLOUR

The crooks' attempt at cooking sets off the alarm, so Ed and his fellow firefighters rush to the pizza parlour. They investigate and quickly realise that there is no fire – only smoke. When they see the crooks are still inside, Ed calls the police. He knows just how to catch the crooks.

I SAW THOSE CROOKS ON TV!

PIZZA PARLOUR

The front of the pizza parlour makes it pretty obvious what's on sale here! There are pizza signs along the top and a wide window showing off the stacked takeaway boxes inside.

Printed pizza tiles attach to angle plates built into the wall.

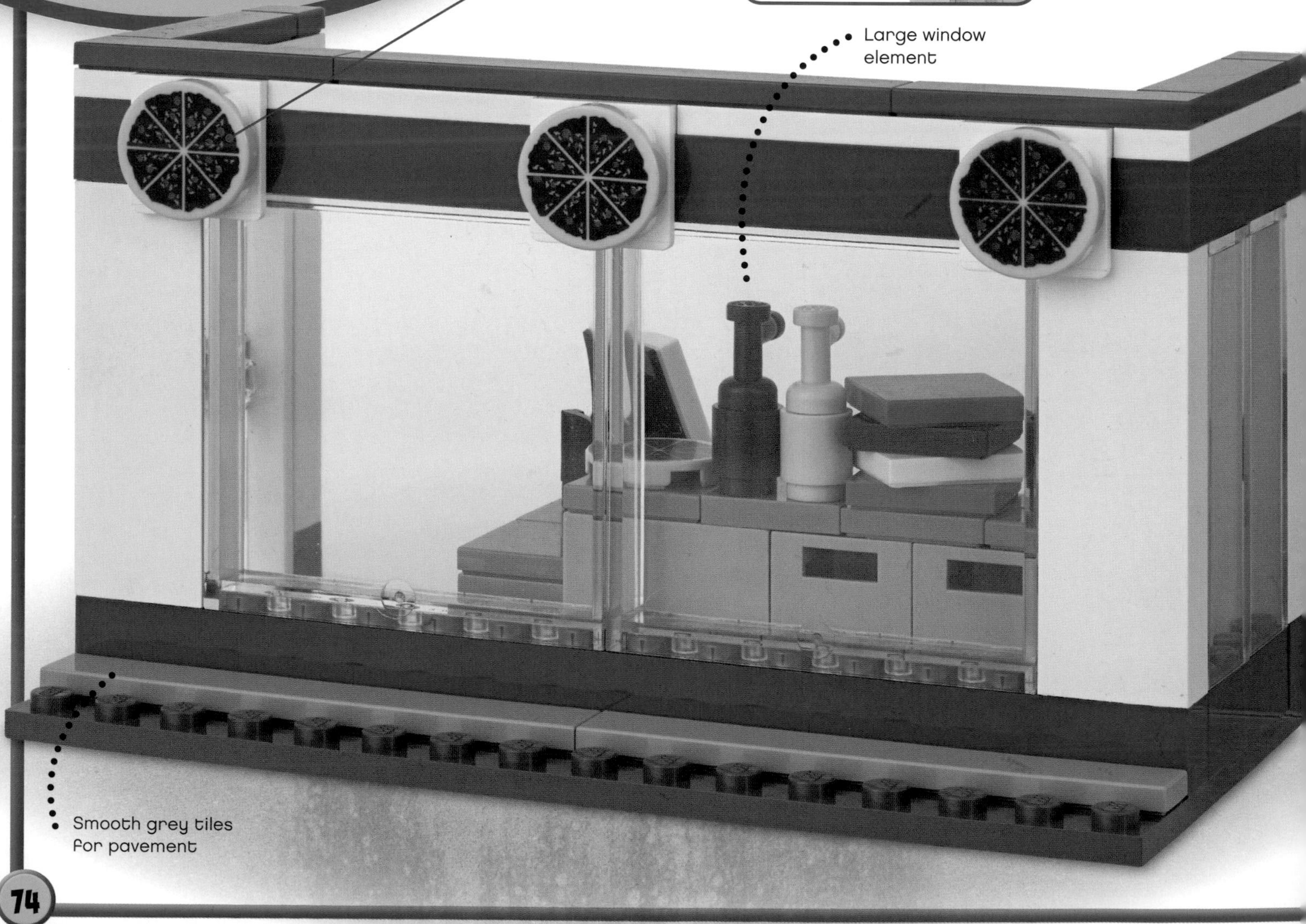

Large window element

Smooth grey tiles for pavement

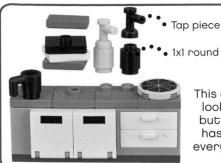

- Tap piece
- 1x1 round brick

This countertop looks smooth, but it actually has studs for every item on it!

SEATING AREA

The crooks don't realise the alarm is ringing in the kitchen. They have moved to the front of the shop where they sit down to eat their pizzas.

REAR VIEW

I'VE GOT A PLAN!

I LIKE STEALING, NOT SHARING.

Cash register is built like the computer on p.28

4x4 round plate tabletop

Plate with angled bars creates the chair's back

WHAT WILL YOU BUILD?
- Supermarket
- Barbershop
- Bank

CRIME SCENE

Ed stretches a safety cordon across the pizza parlour door and calls: "There's a fire! Everybody out!". The crooks run out of the door – and straight into a tangle of tape! A police car and two officers arrive to take the crooks back to jail – where they might eventually get something to eat...

I'VE CAUGHT THEM ED-HANDED!

SAFETY CORDON

Once the crooks are caught, Ed uses stripy incident tape to keep the public away from the scene. It is made from plates with clips and plates with bars so it can flex into different shapes.

WE'RE IN DEEP-PAN TROUBLE.

FRONT VIEW

BUMPER BUILD

You can make a curved bumper out of long, smooth pieces like the curved slope on the bottom of the bumper. Another option is using lots of separate parts, like the slope pieces and grille plate on top.

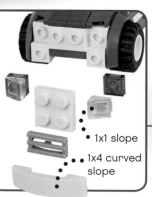

1x1 slope

1x4 curved slope

THAT'S WHAT I CALL A TAKEAWAY.

GREAT WORK, ED.

An upside-down grey angle plate on a 1x2 black tile supports each segment

Transparent blue 1x4 tile makes a strip of lights

1x2 grille plate bumper

Blue sidelights behind headlights

Wheel arch brick protects tyre

POLICE CAR

This rapid-response patrol car is first on the scene after Ed alerts the police. It has space in the back for storing gear and blue emergency lights. The front windscreen piece is more sloped than the rear one, for a more aerodynamic look.

1x1 slope

1x1 corner panel

DOUBLE DOOR

Both sides of the police car are built with a door and side mirror. The door piece sits beside a 1x1 corner panel. Both the door and the mirrors are held in place by the windscreen above.

THE END

It has been a very busy day for Ed. All the people he has helped today have gathered to thank him for his hard work. The only people who aren't welcome are the crooks!

Penguin Random House

Senior Editor Hannah Dolan
Project Art Editor Lauren Adams
Editor Beth Davies
Senior Pre-Production Producer Siu Yin Chan
Senior Producer Louise Daly
Managing Editor Paula Regan
Managing Art Editor Guy Harvey
Art Director Lisa Lanzarini
Publisher Julie Ferris
Publishing Director Simon Beecroft

Written by Simon Hugo
Inspirational models built by Alice Finch
Additional models built by Rod Gillies
Photography by Gary Ombler

Dorling Kindersley would like to thank Randi Sørensen,
Paul Hansford, Martin Leighton Lindhardt, Anette Dall,
Pierre Normandin, Thomas Foli, and Charlotte Neidhardt
at the LEGO Group. Thanks also to Joel Kempson
for editorial assistance and Anne Sharples
for design assistance at DK.

First published in Great Britain in 2016 by
Dorling Kindersley Limited
80 Strand, London WC2R 0RL
A Penguin Random House Company

10 9 8 7 6 5 4
017–288027–Aug/16

Page design copyright © 2016 Dorling Kindersley Limited

A catalogue record for this book is available
from the British Library.

ISBN: 978-0-24123-705-2

Colour reproduction by Tranistics Data Technologies Pvt. Ltd.
Printed and bound in China

www.LEGO.com
www.dk.com

A WORLD OF IDEAS:
SEE ALL THERE IS TO KNOW